A

Meditations to Inspire Compassion, Contemplation, Well-Being & the Spiritual Life

A New Day

Meditations to Inspire Compassion, Contemplation, Well-Being & the Spiritual Life

John Smelcer

Illustrated by Michael T. Duncan

Golden Antelope Press
715 E. McPherson
Kirksville, Missouri 63501
2020

ISBN   978-1-936135-68-4 (1-936135-68-X)

Library of Congress Control Number: 2020932467

Golden Antelope Press
715 E. McPherson
Kirksville, Missouri 63501
www.goldenantelope.com
Phone: (660) 665-0273
Email: ndelmonico@sbcglobal.net

"The Spiritual Life is not merely something to be known and studied; it is to be lived." -Thomas Merton

"The greatest privilege in life is to help awaken the Soul of another." –Plato

The author would like to thank the following individuals for their help: Amber Johnson, Neal and Betsy Delmonico, Rusty Nelson, Steve and Elaine McDuff, Todd Miller, Dale Stone, and Matthew Fox.

For my daughters, Zara and Ayiana—
born a quarter century apart
but always in my heart.

Contents

Foreword

I AM NO SAGE ON A MOUNTAINTOP, no learned hermit in a cave. I began my earnest study of meditation, mindfulness, and world religions at the age of fifty. In that regard, I am unlike the celebrated monks, nuns, and priests who have lived their lives as they preached. But maybe some life-lessons can only be learned after a half century or more of experiencing life. Perhaps that's why sages and philosophers are almost always old. Time is a patient teacher. Like you, I am a product of the increasingly agitated and noisome society in which I exist. Like you, I was caught up in the hurried world of "getting and spending," overwhelmed by life's distractions and intrusions. I was vain and self-centered, thinking the world revolved around me, always singing the Song of Myself. I ate too much fast food. I was always stressed out. I begrudged others for who or what they were. Like you, I wasted my life addicted to social media, the Internet, and television—what one of my teachers called "cultural nerve gas."

Some people who know me might scoff on learning that I have written a book such as this. They would be the first to tell you that I have certainly not lived my life as this book preaches. And they would be correct. In that respect, I am just like you—someone who wants to slow down and get off the endless merry-go-round of "keeping up with the Joneses" and buying things to fill the hollowness inside, someone in search of a better way to live, a better way of Being. Perhaps I wrote this book for myself, for my own edification. But I'm willing to share what I have learned with you. Let's hope it doesn't take you as long as it took me.

It should be stated from the start that some of what I say here is not original. How many ways have we been told to be kind and compassionate, to be still and meditate, to "stop and smell the roses," to unplug, to downsize, to share, to judge less, to forgive, to seek peace and justice, and to be more tolerant and inclusive? Insofar as there is nothing new under the sun, as best I could, I have tried to express my thoughts in original ways. Elsewhere, I have attributed quotes to their sources.

I recommend that you read only a few sayings at a time and contemplate them. Don't just memorize them. Internalize them. Keep this book by your bedside. Read it while walking or sitting in the sun. Take it with you hiking or camping or while sitting on the bus or subway. For the messages of this book to matter, you must be honest with yourself. You must abandon your illusions, your false sense of self and the lies we all tell ourselves. You must come to realize that much of what society imposes on you is also illusion. Only by recognizing these truths can you learn to live joyously and whole. The good news is it is never too late to begin living your life deliberately, mindfully, and compassionately. Every day is a new day.

The Universal Golden Rule

In every major world religion, there is some variation of what has come to be called "The Golden Rule." Perhaps the best explanation for the similarities is that what is advocated is the most fundamental truth of humanity.

Christianity:

"In everything, do to others as you would have them do to you." Jesus, *Matthew* 7:12

Buddhism:

"Do not treat others in ways that you yourself would find hurtful." *Udana Varga* 5.18

Judaism:

"What is hateful to you, do not do to others. This is the whole Torah." Hillel the Elder, *Talmud Shabbat* 31a

Islam:

"Not one of you truly believes until you wish for others what you wish for yourself." The Prophet Muhammad, *Hadith*

Hinduism:

"Do not do to others what would cause pain to you. This is the sum of all duties." *Mahabharata* 5:1517

Confucianism:

"Do not do to others what you do not want done to yourself." Confucius, *Analectics* 15-23

Taosim:

"Regard your neighbor's gain as your gain, and your neighbor's loss as your loss." *T'ai Chang Kan Ying P'ien* 213-218

Jainism:

"One should treat all the creatures of the world as one would like to be treated." Mahavira, *Sutrakri-tanga*

Baha'i:

"Desire not for anyone the things you would not desire for yourself." Baha'u'llah

Sikhism:

"As you deem for yourself, so deem for others."

African Religions (Nigeria):

"Before inflicting harm on any other living being, first inflict it on yourself to feel how much it hurts."

Alaska Native (Ahtna):

"One thing I have learned in my life: Kindness invites kindness and unkindness invites unkindness." Ahtna Athabaskan elder

Our Similarities

Two arms. Two legs. A head with two eyes, a mouth and nose and two ears. A heart, lungs, a duodenum. Even a belly button. Stop seeing other people for their differences and start seeing them for their similarities.

No matter where we live, or what we look like, or what we believe, everyone yearns to be safe and happy.

Love comes in many forms, often mysteriously: romantic love, unrequited love, love of a friend, love of a pet, inter-generational love, brotherly or sisterly love, the love of a daughter who instructs doctors to cease heroic measures to keep her father alive; and even the love of a son who puts his mother into a nursing home against her will when her dementia is so severe that she can no longer live on her own.

There are as many ways to love as there are people in the world.

"In all people I see myself." –Walt Whitman

Around the world and in many cultures, it is said that God sometimes assumes the form of a stranger or beggar, or even appears as a refugee fleeing the threat of violence, economic instability, or famine. God does this in order to witness how we act toward the stranger. Do we mistreat the stranger? Do we turn our backs on the needs of our fellow man? Are we selfish, thinking only of ourselves, or do we aid the stranger without promise of recompense? Too many people ask, "Why should I help those strangers? They are not real people. They do not look like us or act like us or speak like us. God does not love one people more than another or one nation more than another. That is why we must strive to see ourselves and those we love in the faces of strangers, for at one time or another we all plead for God to deliver us from our suffering. We expect God to help us, but God expects us to help one another. That is why we were given two hands to lift up those who have fallen, and two eyes to see the hurt in others so that we can give aid and comfort. God judges each of us by the way we treat others, by our kindness and mercy. Do not to turn away people in need of help, for it may be God testing you.

We are fashioned from a thousand different life experiences. Consequently, no two people see the world in exactly the same way. Therefore, do not condemn those who do not believe things the same way as you do.

To love God and to love other people is the same thing.

"We are all leaves on one tree and drops of one ocean." -Baha'i

"You are not a drop in the ocean. You are the ocean in a drop." -Rumi

It is only with our hearts that we truly see each other. Our eyes can be deceived by color and beauty. If we see one another only with our eyes we are all blind.

When you see yourself in others, it is difficult to hate them.

If God is in each of us, then it is through each other's eyes that we gaze upon God and God gazes upon us.

Break down the stone walls that separate us and build bridges with the stones.

The Spiritual Life

"The Spiritual Life is not merely something to be known and studied; it is to be lived." -Thomas Merton

It has been variously said that God is not a noun, a thing. God is a verb, a call to action—the act of loving and helping others.

What is God if not an irresistible force compelling us toward love?

We are called to be bearers of love for there can be no faith without love.

No hour of life is wasted that is spent loving or serving others.

Meister Eckhart, Thomas Merton, and Dietrich Bonhoeffer all understood that any profession of faith must be bound up with the struggle against injustice and inhumanity. Compassion is the soul in action. Compassion means justice. You must not turn your back on the needs or rights of others. There is no virtue in a hardened heart.

By learning to serve humanity tirelessly and universally, we become a living force for good and justice in an increasingly selfish and weary world.

Anyone who boasts how enlightened they are radiates as much light as an unlit candle in a cave. Humility is a hallmark of enlightenment.

Knowledge of scripture is of no consequence whatsoever. Too many folks spout it out to impress
others, but they do not internalize it, or else they
wouldn't be so prideful. It is the action of loving
others that matters, not empty words blown away
on the wind.

Scripture that is recited without love is soon cov-
ered with dust.

The greatest faith is often forged in the furnace of
doubt. Even the most holy men and women, saints
included, have been filled with doubt. There is no
path to faith without doubt.

Perhaps humanity's greatest capability is our imag-
ination, our curiosity, our desire to know, to learn,

and to understand. Religion and science both endeavor to answer many of the same questions: Who are we? How did we get here? Where is here? What lies beyond here? Both seek to help us understand our place in the universe.

It is not so important that you worship at an altar made of wood or stone or brick or steel, but at the altar of your heart. Because it is said that God dwells in everything and everything dwells in God, it is not the place that matters so much for worship, but the genuine heartfelt love.

What makes us human, you ask? It is not the things we do or the things we build. It is our capability to look inside ourselves and to explore and wrestle with what we find there. Our conscience is what makes us human.

"Cogito, ergo sum. I think, therefore I am."
    —Descartes

It is of no matter what you take into yourself, what you should or should not eat or drink. All that matters is what comes out of you: love, compassion, mercy, charity, patience, and forgiveness. The only things that defile you are hate, intolerance, envy, and selfishness.

Do not be confused by the outward appearances and trappings of being religious: the once-a-week routine of dressing in your "Sunday Best" and then going to church and afterward to lunch with friends or family. God doesn't care about your routine. God cares that you love every single person as much as you love the closest people in your lives.

I watch with amusement as the picnickers in a city park run for cover when a sudden cloudburst erupts. As they flee holding their jackets or books over their heads, I am unable to discern the righteous from the wicked. Those who got drenched certainly did nothing to deserve it. -adapted from a saying from the Wisdom of the Desert Fathers

The next time someone is kicked out of your group, whatever group that may be, because they are imperfect, meaning they may have sinned at some time in their past or are perceived to have sinned, get up and leave with them. When asked why you are leaving, reply that you are not perfect either.

How is it that we think ourselves so perfect and everyone else so imperfect? Nobody is perfect. Love your imperfect neighbor with your imperfect heart.

Freedom means the right to not like the same things: anchovies on pizza, Brussel sprouts, certain films or television shows, broadcast sports, political ideologies or the politicians who propound them.

It is not Fear or Hatred that should reign in the world, but Love.

In our arrogance, we all sing the songs of our self-ishness. But our selfishness imprisons us. Only compassion for others delivers us from the illusion that we are alone and that no one cares for us or loves us.

In our idealized rendering of ourselves as the center of everything, we become immune to all else—ambiguity, irony, hypocrisy, complexity, and most of all other perspectives. We can only contemplate the world one way: with ourselves at the center.

Too many people live by the adage: "Every man for himself." Although God's most ardent desire is that we love one another selflessly, unselfishness is the least enduring of all our capacities.

Thomas Merton once wrote how one day while he was standing on a busy street corner in Louisville, Kentucky, that for a fleeting moment he felt the love that God feels for every single person in that crowded intersection. For that instant he loved every person with the same abiding love. If only we could all live with such a profound realization every day.

Do not wear your devoutness like a medal with which to measure yourself against others, thinking yourself better, for that is vanity and leads to division. Every person comes to God in his or her own way. If you consider yourself more religious than others, you have completely missed the message. It is as if you had never heard it at all.

Being religious doesn't mean one must renounce the world and all its "getting and spending." The purpose of religious life is life.

Let your heartfelt prayer or contemplation be incorporated into everything you do.

There is a chasm between "being religious" and "being righteous," a chasm deeper than any canyon on Earth or abyss beneath the sea. Only the self-righteous and the prideful believe they are one and the same.

Bereft of love, joy, and compassion, piousness and religiousness is nothing but a burden.

Faith, like love, grows by small gestures, not by grand ones.

Fear, Suffering, & Loneliness

So many people suffer from a sense of purpose-lessness, uselessness, and emptiness. "What am I supposed to do with my life? Who am I supposed to be?" Such questions are illusion, promulgated by the corporate notion that a job title on a business card defines your value. It is only a piece of paper.

It's sad that so many people waste their lives trying to "figure out who they are," when all along they were always who they are, for they can be no other. Stop worrying about what other people think about you. Love yourself as you are.

At some point, we all frantically search the road-map of our lives, looking for the X that says, "You are here!"

I'll tell you what I told my adult daughter: There is no road map to life. You're not supposed to be here or there, be this or that, or to have reached some milestone by a certain age. You don't have to earn a degree by twenty-two. You don't have to be a millionaire by thirty. My best friend made this resolution when he was a teenager. He was greatly disappointed on his thirtieth birthday and has considered himself a failure ever since. You don't have to have two new cars and live in an enormous house paying the enormous mortgage that goes with it for the rest of your life. Such things are illusions portrayed by television, movies, and commercials. Don't be a slave to such materialistic stirrings. What matters is finding who you are inside and what makes you happy, no matter your vocation or the size of your house. The important thing is not where you end up in life; it is that you ever lived at all.

People always worry which path they should take in life. They worry that this path or that path may lead to failure. The truth is every path leads to you. We are each made into who we are by our life experiences, including our most spectacular failures.

Too many people pray to avoid suffering, but it is only from experiencing suffering that we learn humility, compassion, and mercy.

Learn to accept that your life will have moments of sadness, disappointment, anxiety, despair, and suffering. Avoid dwelling on these emotions. Every person on Earth—rich, famous, or destitute—experiences all these emotions at one time or another.

So much of our fears are illusion—fear of moving to a new town; fear of going to college; fear of letting go of something or someone. Fear is a tyrant.

Clinging too tightly to anything leaves claw marks when you are finally forced to let go.

Our own suffering is diminished when we give solace to others who are in need or suffering. Our sadness opens us up to each other.

Where there is a person who is lonely or hurting, there is a chance for compassion.

It has been variously said that the opposite of love is not hate but indifference. Do not be indifferent to the suffering or needs of others. Indifference gives rise to atrocities and tragedies, large and small.

All your anxiety and worrying doesn't really exist. The birds don't see it. That squirrel beside a tree doesn't see it. The sun comes up and down every day without concern. Your own mind creates much of your suffering. Stop thinking your problems are bigger than they are and they may vanish altogether.

It has been variously said that happiness is not about a place you arrive at. It's about the journey. You won't be happy once you arrive someplace if you weren't happy along the way.

Avoid criticizing yourself and thinking that you are a failure or that your life is meaningless. At the same time, do not criticize or judge others.

A priest friend once told me that it's impossible to feel sad when you're eating ice cream. It turns out he was right.

Dwelling on the past too much is not conducive to happiness. You cannot change the past, no matter how fervently you wish you could. Herodotus said that you can never step into the same river twice. Even if you stood at the exact same spot a minute later, the river is no longer the same. Thousands of gallons of water have already flowed by. Sand and pebbles have slipped downstream. Fish that had been here are now there. The shadow of a cloud on the surface has moved. Learn from your mistakes, but don't let them consume you.

Accept the past as that which has already happened without denying it or trying to run from it or discarding it—none of which is possible.

Although there is only this moment, the ghosts of our past are always with us, for good or bad. The key to wholeness is learning how to balance the paradox.

The past has no power over the present. Yesterday is nothing more than a memory, synapses fired by electrical impulses. Worse yet, neuroscientists have learned that a good deal of our memories is incomplete and inaccurate, even fabricated. Treat each new day as a separate life.

To paraphrase Emily Dickinson: "Forever is a series of infinite and fleeting nows."

Some folks believe they are masters of their lives and that they control the future. In their self-centeredness, they think they are like bulldozers forcing their will on the world, but we are more like feathers carried on a river.

The same priest, who taught me about the joy of eating ice cream, once reminded me: "Man makes plans. God laughs." Perhaps he was familiar with Thomas Kempis's "Man proposes; God disposes." And perhaps that's why Scottish poet Robert Burns once wrote, "Even the best-laid plans of mice and men often go awry" (from "To a Mouse").

I had a friend who retired, sold her house, moved across the country to be closer to her children and grandchildren, and died unexpectedly a year later of an embolism. I imagine we all know someone like that: a parent, friend, co-worker, or neighbor. Life is unpredictable. Thinking we have any control over it is illusion.

"Not being able to govern the future, I govern myself." -Montaigne

Hope waits on the other side of despair. I know this to be true as much as I know that gravity holds my feet to the Earth. My younger brother, James Ernest, did not know this truth. He committed suicide in 1988 at the age of 22 because he could not see the light through the darkness.

Sometimes a drop of happiness is enough to stave off a sea of despair.

Faith and Hope: the names of two ships that dare the future and brave the sea of uncertainty.

Hope cannot exist without faith. Faith cannot exist without love.

Lao-Tzu, the ancient Chinese philosopher and author of the *Tao Te Ching* once said, "If you never expect results from actions you will never be disappointed."

When I was a boy, I was riding my bicycle too fast around a sharp turn strewn with gravel. Needless to say, I crashed scraping my hands, elbows, and knees. After that, I learned to slow down on curves. Fifty years later, I still watch for loose gravel on the road when I ride my motorcycle. Every great lesson I have ever learned came from failure.

Our failures and mistakes help us to grow and to mature. To alleviate suffering in yourself and in others, practice compassion, forgiveness, and mercy.

Too many people suffer from feelings of unutterable and alienating loneliness.

Recent surveys show a higher score of social isolation (loneliness) among Generation Z (pre-teens, tweens, and teens) compared to participants aged 72 or older. It is worthwhile to consider why the most plugged-in group is the loneliest.

The population of every country grows by millions every year, and yet people are lonelier than. Could it be that media and advertisements have filled us with false perceptions of who or what we should be looking for?

Every person is deserving of being loved. Every person is capable to giving love.

So many people are lonely nowadays. Try as they may, they are unable to find someone to be loved by. But consider this: while you may dip a cup into the middle of the sea and not catch a single fish, yet we all know the sea is full of fish.

Fear has held back so many people from realizing their potential. "I'm afraid." "What if?" Fear is a normal, even necessary response. We all feel afraid at times. Why do you get scared at the top of a high ladder or on a rooftop? Answer: Because you could fall and hurt yourself. Fear encourages precaution. Have the courage to accept your feelings for what they are, yet to be brave enough not to allow those feelings to hinder your dreams and aspirations.

"If you don't risk anything, you risk even more."
-Marianne Moore

Courage is not the absence of fear. It's being absolutely afraid, but facing the moment or embracing the opportunity despite the uneasy feeling.

Your courage can inspire others. Sometimes all people need is the example of a single act of courage in the face of overwhelming fear.

We don't grieve simply because we miss someone in our life. We grieve to heal.

Paycheck by paycheck and raise after raise, we abandon our old dreams.

In our consumerist culture of entitlement and instant gratification where we think money can buy us anything, too many people battle against aging and dying, a war they can never win. Learn to accept that death is part of life and strive instead to live more fully.

Less is More

I'm always dismayed at how many people pay for storage units to store the things they obviously can live without. Month after month, year after year, they pay thousands of dollars to store the overflow and detritus of their consumerist lives. I once paid $7,000 over five years for a storage unit that was crammed full of things I thought I couldn't live without. There were dozens of boxes of books I had not opened in a decade. One day, I finally tossed it all out, but the silly manager of the storage unit didn't refund all the money I had paid to him over the years. Think of what I could have done with all that money! I could have taken an amazing vacation or fed a hundred children for three months. Many of us are in the same boat. Owning things will never make you happy.

Some time ago, my wife decided that we had too much stuff. She started to systematically down-size our household possessions, donating anything we hadn't used in over a year or which did not bring us joy to own. "What about this?" she asked, holding up some object. "What about that?" she said, pointing to another. I resisted at first, even to the suggestion of discarding or donating things I hadn't used in years, like my dust-covered Swiss fondue pot (Oh, the fond memories of the 1970s). I culled my CD and DVD collections (but not my Tony Orlando & Dawn and The Partridge Family albums), the number of books on shelves; the number of neck ties hanging in my closet (there were over 100). The result of my wife's efforts is that our lives are less cluttered and happier. From the experience, I understand why monks and nuns take vows of poverty. Their lives are not impover-ished for lack of things. To the contrary!

Jesus told his would-be disciples to leave everything behind if they wanted to follow him. Some followed; others did not. Likewise, The Buddha left the riches and splendor of palace life behind. Materialism and consumerism impede the growth of the Soul, for they are all about the Self.

Strive to possess nothing, the entirety of it.

Happiness is letting go of what you don't need.

The love of money conquers all other loves until nothing remains but all-consuming greed.

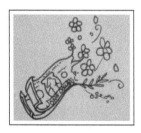

There are many addictions. Always wanting more is one of them. Buying things will never make you happy for long.

According to National Geographic, the Environmental Protection Agency and numerous other organizations, 90% of everything we buy ends up in a landfill within a year (think of all the packaging material alone).

Too many young folks nowadays pray for riches, success, and fame—all contrary to the things that will truly make you happy.

The average size of an American home in 1950 was 1,000 square feet. Today, that number is almost tripled at 2,600. Human beings haven't gotten any larger as a species since 1950, nor has family size, only our environmental footprint.

Our national anthem: "More, more, more! Bigger, bigger, bigger!"

I know a man who paid off his twenty year mortgage when he retired. But instead of enjoying the rest of his life mortgage-free, he took out a second mortgage that would take another twenty years to pay off. He bought a new truck, a motorhome, and a house full of new, expensive designer furniture. He paid to have his shower renovated in Italian marble. A few years later, all of those things had depreciated greatly in value, yet he will be stuck paying off the loan until he dies. When I asked him why he did it, he replied, "Because it's the American Way to be in debt. It's good for the economy."

Consumerism is an insatiable hunger that devours everything. "I want!" it cries out in its gluttony. "More!" it screams from the precipice as the last tree is cut and the last fish is hoisted from the empty sea.

A sign on the wall in a Big Box chain store: "You really can buy happiness." Rubbish!

The motto of Materialism: "Mine! Mine! Mine!"

All around the world, species are being driven to extinction, in part because we are destroying entire ecosystems in our insatiable and ever-increasing greed for resources. Our wholesale destruction of the world may eventually bring about our own extinction. Some people say we can just move to other planets and other solar systems. Who do you think would be onboard those rocket ships, the poor who could not afford the cost, or the rich who profited by plundering the planet in the first place? Before we plunge humanity into the abyss of space to eke out a living on distant worlds, why not simply try to preserve this planet? Have compassion for the Earth.

"Do not destroy what you cannot create."
    —Leo Szilard

More than anyone else, it was famed astronomer Carl Sagan who convinced NASA to turn around the camera on Voyager at the end of its mission when it was four billion miles from home to take a picture of Earth. The iconic image of our planet as a pale blue dot no larger than a single pixel in a shaft of sunlight showed just how small, fragile and unique our planet really is.

Some people believe that God made the world as a gift for humanity. If you say you love God, why don't you protect the world God made? Do you think God will make another one? Wasn't one miracle sufficient?

In profound selfishness, Americans proclaim they will never allow our "Way of Life" to be impacted by the world's ever-decreasing resources. "We have the right to own all the gas-guzzling SUV's and energy-wasting McMansions we want and to waste more food than any other nation on Earth!" At the same time, America has more nuclear missiles than any other country. Pity the rest of the world that needs the same resources to exist!

The United Nations predicts the world population will be ten billion or more by 2050 based on mortality rates and growth experienced over the past century. Further, they predict 70% of all humanity will live in cities and that there will be at least thirty megacities with populations exceeding thirty million. If we can't get along in a world of seven billion people, how will we ever get along in a world of ten billion?

Three billion more people in the future means three billion more mouths to feed, a billion more cars on the road, and a billion more homes that need electricity and gas to heat and cool. It also means billions more cell phones, and cheap plastic products sold at Big Box megastores. The world's resources are already dangerously depleted. What will the future hold if we don't change our ways?

Do you want to be happier? Do you feel your life has no purpose other than going to work, buying stuff, and going back to work the next day just to pay off debt? Stop buying stuff.

Corporate America has purposefully married Christianity to Capitalism, trying to make you believe God wants you to be rich and to have lots of stuff. It falsely tries to convince you that America's Gross Domestic Product is proof that God loves America more than any other nation or people in the world.

In America, politicians have declared that corporations have the same rights as human beings. I wonder: Do they have souls? By equating corporations with people, what new meaning is assigned to the phrase in the Constitution, "We the People"? The bottom line of most corporations is greed—the making of profit at all costs. As children, we are admonished by our parents, "Don't be so greedy!" Where is it written that greed is a virtue?

Benjamin Franklin, one of America's Founding Fathers famously said, "Time is money," implying that time exists only for the purpose of working to make money. What a sad thought.

Millionaire TV Evangelists wearing $25,000 suits and sporting $50,000 wristwatches with gold and

diamond rings on every finger arrive at their mul-
timillion dollar megachurch on Sunday morning
in limousines. When these preachers are asked
about their fabulous display of wealth they reply,
"God wants me to be rich." Where in the Gospels
does it say to be rich and to possess lots of things?
In fact, Jesus said, "It is harder for a rich man to
enter the Kingdom of Heaven than to thread a
camel through the eye of a needle" (Mark 10:25,
Matthew 19:24) and, "You cannot have two masters," the love for money and the love for others
(Matthew 6:24). These warning echoes in the Talmud: "Anyone who uses the scriptures to gain
wealth will perish." "The Gospel of Prosperity" is
a false prophet.

Love for the welfare of others must trump the love
of money.

Too many people pray, "Please, Lord, let me win
the lottery just one time." You should know that
no prayer made at the Altar of Greed is ever an-
swered.

This morning I placed a pile of bird seed on my
back porch. I watched as one little bird bullied all
the other little birds from coming to the pile, which

was a mountain compared to him. He couldn't possibly eat it all those seeds in a year. Don't be like that greedy little bird.

Later that morning, I heard on public radio a story about a marine biologist who was swimming among a pod of whales when a large whale came right at her and started pushing her away. Although frightened, the woman was not harmed, only shaken from the experience. From her new vantage point, a safe distance from where she had been, she saw that the whales were driving away an enormous tiger shark. The whales had protected the woman from the shark. Be like the whale.

Digital Detox

As a cultural anthropologist and astute observer of the contemporary social scene, I can attest that we are all victims of our society—the insidious and relentless advertisements and television programs that tell us what to buy, how to look and dress; that tell us we will finally be happy if only we bought this or that product; and the news soundbytes and talk shows that tell us what to think. By spreading disinformation, our smartphones have become Weapons of Mass Deception. Thousands of times a day, we are bombarded by illusions created by people who do not have our best interest at heart.

Recognize that your desire to "fit in" is a powerful sociological force. We all want to belong. But be leery of what you are trying to belong to.

Reducing things in your life is not the only way to happiness. Reducing "screen time" has been shown to increase happiness.

They say the average American sees 5,000 advertisements per day. That's 1.8 million per year! I would say that holds true in much of the developed world nowadays. (Ever see a photo of downtown Tokyo or Times Square?) All those advertisements only serve to confuse you and to tell you who and what you should be.

In 1968, during a religious conference at Our Lady of Redwoods monastery in Northern California, Thomas Merton told the participants, "The wrong idea of personal fulfillment is promoted by commercialism. Advertisements try to sell things which none of us would buy in our right mind; so they keep us in our wrong mind. There is a kind of self-fulfillment that fulfils nothing but your illusory self. What truly matters is not how to get the most out of life, but how to recollect yourself so that you can fully give yourself."

I recently attended an event for college students. I was stunned when I looked around at all the students sitting together at tables—four here, two or three there—all facing each other, yet not one person was talking to another. Every single person was on their phone checking social media and messages.

You may not be old enough to remember, but it wasn't too long ago that there was no such thing as the Internet or email or cell phones. I grew up before all that new technology. The Internet didn't exist until I was in college. Back then, we checked our mailbox once a day to see if we got any messages (letters). But nowadays, people are obsessed with how many messages they get.

They neurotically check their email or social media messages dozens of times a day, some more than 150 times a day. That's 54,000 times a year! Is it so important that "friends" you may have never met tell you or show you what they ate for lunch or the artfully crafted cup of coffee they had at a coffee house? Can you live without the funny joke or funny picture someone shared on the Internet?

It has been reported that social media designers purposely created "likes" to addict you to their product or service in the same way that cigarette manufacturers purposely added nicotine to addict users. They use psychology to devise ways to make you unwittingly browse more frequently and longer on a webpage, which translates into more money via advertising sales for the social platform.

Psychologists have found that using social media releases Dopamine, the same neurotransmitter chemical related to reward-motivated behavior that makes us addicted to smoking, drinking, or gambling. Social media designers know it, too.

As proof that cell phones and social media are addictive, it was reported in 2019 that P. Diddy, the popular American rapper and songwriter, checked himself into an addiction center because of his obsession with his smart phone. He purportedly checked his phone over 600 times a day. That's every 1.5 minutes during the waking day. That's 18,000 times a month and over 200,000 times a year!

It amazes me how many people say, "I don't have time in my busy life for this or that," but they find hours and hours each day to read and post on social media, to aimlessly browse the Internet, or to binge-watch mindless television. Just put down your smartphone. Turn it off. Unplug. Walk away.

Andy Warhol once said that every person gets fifteen minutes of fame in their life. Nowadays, because of the Internet and social media, people want their fifteen minutes of fame every single day. "I have hundreds of friends!" they gleefully exclaim while swallowing an antidepressant pill prescribed for depression caused by loneliness.

I used to teach a popular university literature course in a packed auditorium. As I circulated around the cavernous hall looking over students' shoulders, I noticed that half of them were checking social media instead of paying attention to class. And that was ten years ago!

All my life I have stood up to bullies, even when they were bigger than me. Sometimes I gave the lumps and sometimes I took my lumps. But I always stood up to injustice and cruelty no matter the outcome. I eventually became a world-class weightlifter so I would be stronger and better able to defend others. Sadly, I have yet to discover a way to stand up against the devastating anonymity of online bullying.

How liberating it was to turn off my Facebook and Twitter accounts and to start living again. I even found myself checking my email less and less each day. What's that warm, bright light shining in the sky? The sun, you say.

Compassion, Joy & Laughter

When questioned about his religion, His Holiness the Dalai Lama once replied, "My religion is kindness." As surely as everything spoils and decays, so too does your heart if you do not use it for kindness and compassion.

Only love for others makes us real. Love and compassion for others is the purest essence of the human spirit.

Researchers conducting MRI brain scans of participants found that altruistic acts, that is, selfless generosity, lights up the subgenual anterior cingulate cortex, one of the brain's reward areas. It turns out that doing something nice for other people with no expectation of a return favor is actually good for us.

Love is the great good use we make of one another.

Love is the most profound creative force in humanity.

See the world through love and the world will be new.

Love is two people, hand in hand, facing the uncertain future together, joyous in the certainty they will not face it alone.

Don't receive strangers closed-handed and closed-hearted, but with open hands and open hearts.

Sometimes the only way to find happiness is to stop looking for it.

Love often arrives unexpectedly, like a stranger at your doorstep.

If you really want to be loved by others, love others first.

If a smile is disarming in every language and culture, laughter unites our humanity.

"Sometimes your joy is the source of your smile, but sometimes your smile is the source of your joy." –Thich Nhat Hanh

The wisest people have one thing in common: they smile often.

You've heard the old saying, "Laughter is the best medicine." It turns out that it's actually true. Laughter heals us physically and emotionally, even spiritually.

Laughter optimizes blood flow by 20%.

With every smile or scowl, every kindness or cruelty, every act of compassion or selfishness, we make ourselves into who we are.

Don't let your spirit be like a frightened bird fluttering in a windowless heart. Open your heart. Let your spirit soar.

Day by day and hour by hour, from a thousand little acts of kindness, we fill ourselves with good.

Justice, Mercy & Forgiveness

It is never God's mercy that is absent from the world, but humanity's ... always humanity's.

It is by love and by love alone that God judges us.

Let your compassion and mercy shine as constant as the stars.

If you are without mercy for others, how can you
expect anyone to be merciful to you? Mercy con-
firms our humility, our humanity, and even the
divinity that is within each of us. Thomas Aquinas
wrote: "Mercy is the fulfillment of justice, not its
denunciation." You can be just and merciful at the
same time. Don't love your man-made laws more
than the sinner who was made by God and who
God loves still and completely. Too often, as an
individual is condemned to die, we say pitilessly,
"May God have mercy on your soul." And yet, the
real question is, why have we shown no mercy
whatsoever? We are closest to God when we show
mercy.

Mercy, like love, has the power to transform the
world.

Love kindness and humility. Strive for peace in all things. Forgive others, for there can be no peace without forgiveness.

Yes, it is true that it is wrong to break the laws. But it is equally true that the greater crime is committed by those who uphold the laws to their fullest in the disposition of punishment without some measure of compassion for the human being. Imposition of law must be imbued with mercy.

Justice and Mercy: The one exalts the other.

"Earthly power does then show like God's when mercy seasons justice."
    –Portia in *The Merchant of Venice*

Those who show no mercy, only cruelty, are incapable of looking into the mirror and recognizing their own transgressions and sins. And if they have, then they lie to themselves about what they have seen slouching there in the darkness. To forgive another person's wrongdoing is to recognize that you are also capable of wrongdoing.

People who do not expect to receive mercy or compassion from others eventually lose their inclination to grant it to others.

When you forgive others it is really yourself you save. Hate is a terrible burden.

"To err is human, to forgive divine."
        —Alexander Pope

"Forgiveness is a virtue of the brave."
  –Indira Gandhi

It is the sin that must die, never the sinner. God commanded, "Do not kill." Do you hold your fleeting man-made laws to be above God's? Mercy also means clemency.

Carl Sagan once wrote, "If a human disagrees with you, let him live. In a hundred billion galaxies you will not find another like him."

Even the greatest saints were sinners.

A world without truth or hope or love is a world in which fear and desire will rule.

A spirit destitute of hope is a poor political adviser, which explains why so many politicians say what you want to hear, even when their actions demonstrate that they have no intention of remedying that which created your hopelessness.

Demanding obedience at all costs, evil seeks to maintain power by suppressing freedom and truth.

Hate cannot flourish without willing followers. Only compassion defeats hate.

You take it for granted that God is merciful and forgiving to you, yet you deny it for others. What monumental arrogance!

Mercy exists because of our imperfections.

Not too long ago, a powerful world leader was asked which biblical trait he most identified with. His answer: Revenge. Pity it wasn't compassion, tolerance, mercy, forgiveness, or peace.

Nothing hardens the heart as much as the desire for revenge.

"When you set off for revenge, first dig two graves."
    —Confucius

Silence, Prayer & Contemplation

True prayer is the surrender of heart and mind un-embellished by the lies we tell ourselves about ourselves. In this way, and only in this way, do our prayers tend toward God's Grace.

The efficacy of prayer lies in suppressing our egos.

Our journey through life will not take us far in the world unless we learn to reflect on the world within.

Prayer and contemplation are not about learning to control one's self, but about learning to let go of one's self, an abandonment of our many attachments. You possess everything only when you possess nothing.

Meditation creates a quiet recess for your unsettled mind to be purged of everyday distractions that assail it. Devoid of such distractions, your mind is like a mirror infinitely reflecting back upon itself.

Just as we can gaze at the seemingly infinite universe through a telescope, so too can we gaze inside ourselves and see a seemingly infinite universe. Shakespeare knew this to be true when he wrote in *Hamlet*: "I could be bounded in a nutshell and count myself a king of infinite spaces." (Act 2, Scene ii)

"Nothing inspires me with as much awe: the starry heavens above, the moral laws within."
    —Immanuel Kant

Learn to be still enough to hear the quiet voice of compassion in your heart, so that you can hear it in others.

In the quiet recess of solitude can be found one's true self, unfettered by deception.

All my life I have been terrified of silence and of being alone. Just ask anyone who knows me. How delightful it was when I learned after more than half a century how unlonely both can be.

Silence and stillness nourishes and revives the weary soul. The noise and hustle-bustle of our busy lives incinerates it.

Sitting still, eyes closed, breathing slowed, restless mind clearing—the hurried world evaporates and another, less hurried world emerges as if from a lifting fog.

You can only hear that small, quiet voice inside your head or heart when you have learned to silence the cacophony outside.

Noise. Noise. Noise. Talk. Talk. Talk. How different the world would be if we learned to love silence as much as we love noise.

For years, I walked down to a creek every day and sat on a log and did nothing. For that is what it must have seemed to a casual observer. Although it may have appeared outwardly as if nothing was happening, everything was happening inside me.

A deliberate, mindful stroll in nature does wonders for the weary soul.

There is an ineffable eloquence to silence.

Doctors are increasingly prescribing time in Nature as a remedy for stress.

We marvel at magnificent vistas, yet we fail to see the beauty within.

The Sufi mystic and poet Rumi once wrote that he wanted to know the secrets of the world, to which God replied, "Let silence tell you the secrets of the world."

I once watched a wounded deer sit for days until she healed. Like the deer, our bodies heal in the silence of stillness and sleep. If you want to heal your body or spirit, go into silence.

There can be no peace or harmony within yourself or with others without first examining your own attitudes, prejudices, and ideals. If you can't find peace in yourself, you can't find peace anywhere.

Let your silent contemplation be fearless when it comes to self-examination. Search your heart for the sources of your alienation, loneliness, selfishness, jealousy, and anger.

Through prayer and contemplation you strive to find God's grace, but in the process you may find it in yourself to become more capable of giving grace to others.

While giving a talk at Redwoods during his last days in America, Thomas Merton insisted, "Nothing that anyone says is that important. The great thing is prayer—prayer itself. If you want a life of prayer, the way to get to it is by praying."

'In prayer we discover what we already have. You start where you are and you deepen what you already have, and you realize that you are already there.' Brother David Steindl-Rast, who attended Thomas Merton's talk at Redwoods in 1968

Faith & Violence

Nationalistic, political, and even religious zealotry blots out conscience and morality.

Blind obedience is about closedness, not openness. Fanaticism makes you blind and deaf to mercy and love. Without conscience or compassion, patriotism, nationalism, and religion are ruthless beasts.

Albert Einstein, who escaped Hitler's gas chambers and ovens, knew this to be true when he wrote: "The greatest obstacle to world peace is that monstrously exaggerated spirit of nationalism, which also goes by the fair-sounding name of patriotism. It seriously threatens the survival of civilization and our very existence. Only by over-coming our national egotism will we be able to contribute towards improving the lot of humanity."

Considering oneself superior to others—either in-dividually or nationalistically—is the root cause of most atrocities against humanity.

Our humanity perishes by our hate and prejudice, injustice and alienation, impoverishment and dis-enfranchisement, violence and war, and every other act of oppression and inhumanity.

"Groups tend to be less guided by conscience than individuals. It is the cause of wars and every kind of oppression, which fill the Earth with pain, sighs, and bitterness."
     —Albert Einstein

Beware of any individual or group that calls them-selves "patriots" and labels those who disagree with them as "unpatriotic," "traitors," or "Enemies of the People." Freedom means the liberty to have different opinions and beliefs and to freely and peaceably express them.

Conformity annihilates individuality.

Being religious can turn even the kindest heart into a heart of stone, in spite of the reasons you give when you set off to "find religion" in the first place. Membership in a religious group or community often encourages comparing yourself to others, measuring your religiousness against theirs, which ultimately leads to judging, one of the pitfalls of pride. Thomas Merton, one of the most influential theological and spiritual thinkers of the last century, and more recently, Rabbi Jonathon Sacks of England both pointed out that one consequence of group identity is that it leads to a Us versus Them or We versus They mentality: We are good and righteous. They are evil and godless sinners. We alone have the true knowledge. They are deceivers. Such group-think leads to prejudice, alienation, dehumanization, and oppression—harbingers of violence.

It is too easy to say that our adversaries are all wicked, sinful, immoral, and deserving of our hatred. No religion or social system is so evil that its people must be considered as without virtue or any redeeming humanity.

Albert Einstein once said, "The world will not be destroyed by those who do evil, but by those who look on without doing anything." Martin Luther King, Jr. called it "the appalling silence of good people."

There can be no love without freedom. Even the choice to love God must come freely and without duress. You cannot compel others to love God, just as you cannot compel others to love you.

Some people use fear to sow discord and divisiveness, for they know that fear is like a contagion. But hope is equally infectious.

Peace triumphs when the love of power yields to the power of love.

Peace fails when listening and understanding fails.

There can be no peace between individuals, groups, or nations without first examining our own attitudes, prejudices, ideologies, and arrogances.

It is written and sung that God knew you in the womb (Jeremiah 1:5, et al). Therefore, God knew who and what you would become and loves you all the same. It is not up to you to decide who is worthy of love.

I know a woman—very close to me—who for years attended what I shall call the First Church of Everytown. One day, a co-worker invited her to attend a picnic that Sunday at her church: the Second Church of Everytown, so named because it was built on the other side of town a few years after the first one was built. They were the same denomination. Two weeks later, when the woman returned to the First Church of Everytown, the congregants kicked her out of their church. "You are against us if you are with them," they decried as they shut the door.

Every adherent of every religion will tell you that God's Nature is absolutely transcendent and unknowable and that we cannot possibly fathom the infinite Mystery of God. Meister Eckhart wrote that God's Mystery "never was known, and never will be known." And yet, it is astonishing how many of those same folks will tell you that only they and their religious group has the truth about God.

One day during the wars in Iraq and Afghanistan, I was sitting in a church waiting for the service to begin when the man sitting beside me on the pew leaned over and whispered, "I say we nuke all those Middle Eastern ragheads. Blast them all to hell—every man, woman, and child." I'm sure he meant to say human beings instead of the demeaning ethnic slur. He must have forgotten that Jesus was a Middle Easterner, as were Mary and Joseph, whose life-sized statues stood to the left and right of the one depicting Jesus on the Cross. A few minutes later, the priest began his homily: "Thou shalt not kill. So sayeth the Lord." To which the congregation—the man sitting beside me included—responded in one voice, "The Word of the Lord."

Ten years later in 2017 (America still embroiled in Afghanistan), I was sitting at a local café in the Midwest where I write every morning, when I overheard a man at a nearby table say, "Hell, I'd shoot all them immigrants myself—men, women, and children. They're all rapists, murderers, and drug dealers. Yes sir, just line 'em up and shoot every one of them." It was Sunday morning. I knew from past experience that the men at that table were on their way to church. The hypocrisy is that the populace of Central/South America is more Christian than the populace of the United States. According to the Association of Religion Archives (2018), 92% of Central/South Americans are Christian. The only possible excuse for such a heinous statement by the man at the table was the color of skin. Racism is always at the heart of such hate, whether we admit it or not.

Our humanity is diminished when others are humiliated, demonized, or diminished. No one lifts themselves up by putting others down.

Real communication and understanding is impossible when we love our ideology more than we love each other.

So many people have been oppressed, enslaved, tortured, and killed in the Name of God. Yet, every major religion teaches that humanity can never know the name of God. Meister Eckhart wrote that "Whatever one says God is, God is not that." St. Augustine wrote of the increasingly mythical concept of God, "If you can comprehend it, it is not God." Saint Thomas Aquinas wrote that "God is an unnameable nothingness." In Hinduism, it is said that we cannot name God (Brahman) for God is neti neti: "Not this, not this." Buddhists caution of the "unknowability of God." In Taoism, Lao-Tzu speaks of the "seamless unnamable." Zen master Thich Nhat Hanh says, "It is impossible to use our concepts and words to describe God." Perhaps the best thing a person can say about God is to say nothing at all.

"When those who love God try to talk about God, their words are like blind lions looking for a spring in a desert."
    —Leon Bloy

Since it is impossible to know the Name of God, perhaps we should stop oppressing and injuring others in the name of God.

I once passed a church. The enormous sign out front said, "A child is like a train. When it goes off track, it's time to use the switch." I couldn't believe it. Here was a church telling people to use violence against children. This is how the never-ending cycle of violence begins. I come from a cultural tradition where children are never physically punished for their mistakes. I have raised two wonderful and thoughtful daughters without having ever once laid a hand on them in anger.

There's more hell in war than all the individual horrors put together. In War of the Worlds, H. G. Wells wrote, "If we do not end war, war will end us." Every war comes to an end, one way or another, win, lose, or draw. No war lasts forever. Only war itself endures. Peace cannot be sustained by guns and tanks and bombers and nuclear missiles. What future is there in devastation? How is annihilation good for the future? Violence begets violence. We delude ourselves if we believe otherwise.

Does might make right? How many nuclear missiles does it take for a nation to be righteous? On which side of the killing field does God stand? At the point when Germany realized it was losing WWII, one German general declared, "The Gods of war have changed sides." He was wrong. God was never on either side. There is no God in killing people.

"Only the dead have seen the end of war."
  —Plato

War exists because nations and individuals seek their own wretched momentary advantage and refuses to subordinate it to the welfare and prosperity of others. The way to joy and peace is through renunciation and self-limitation in all things.

Peace is the most desperate need of humanity, yet it is also the most unattainable.

War rips away all vestiges of morality and compassion. The overpowering greed to survive at any cost, no matter how many others you kill, eventually leads to atrocities against humanity.

The end never justifies the means. Not even with regards to religion—especially with regards to religion.

The Things Walter Taught Me

Walter Charley, a renowned Alaska Native wisdom teacher of Native Ways of Knowing, was my spiritual mentor up until his death in 1992. He was related to me through my full-blood Indian grandmother. Throughout my years as a student at the University of Alaska Fairbanks, which spanned the entire 1980s, I used to drive down to our village to learn from him. One fall evening, he told me the following story while we were sitting around a campfire:

A man wanted to learn how to control his anger, which was so frightful even grizzly bears feared him. He was always getting into fights whenever he perceived that someone had insulted him. Just a look could set him off. A shaman told him to insult and beat a log with a stick until he was exhausted. Shortly thereafter, sweating from his prodigious labor, the man asked the shaman, "What lesson was I supposed to learn from beating a log?" To which the shaman replied, "Be like the log."

One summer day Walter and I took a walk along the road outside his village. When a car passed by the driver shouted something cruel at us. I gave him the finger. Walter grabbed my upraised hand and gently pulled it down. "I have observed that kindness brings kindness and unkindness brings unkindness."

Walter and I were walking down a trap-line trail in the middle of winter when we saw a wolverine loping through the snow. Although they are much smaller than bears, wolverines have a reputation as the fiercest of animals. They are extremely elusive. In a lifetime of living in the wilds of Alaska, I have only seen a wolverine on one other occasion. Always ready to take advantage of a teaching moment, Walter turned to me.

"Did you know there are two wolverines inside you?"

He was always saying things like that.

"Um, no," I replied reticently.

"They live here," he said, stabbing my head with a gloved finger. "They are always fighting for control of your feelings. One is good. Its nature is love, kindness, generosity, empathy, humility, and compassion."

I nodded as if I understood.

"You say you understand, but you are too young to understand such things," said my mentor in the way that he always corrected me.

"The other is bad. Its nature is anger and hate, greed and arrogance, jealousy, envy, fear and violence."

We walked on in silence, the only sound snow crunching beneath our boots. Finally, I stopped and stood in the middle of the trail.

"Which one wins?" I asked.

Walter looked me in the eyes.

"The one you feed," he said.

[I have since learned that variations of this story are told across Native America.]

Sitting in his warm cabin during the coldest time of the year, Walter told me that there is nothing wrong with folks seeing things differently. We do not all have to be the same to get along. "It is okay to be different," he said. "To have peace, it is not necessary for eagles to become ravens."

Although my tribe hunts for food, Walter always taught me to have compassion for animals. In my half century of living in Alaska, I risked my life to rescue moose calves drowning in raging rivers after their heavier and stronger mothers safely forged across to the other side. The first time was on the Goodpaster River. The last time was on the upper Klutina River. As I was walking back to my second cousin's truck, sopping wet, cold, and beaming ear-to-ear with joy, the little moose calf I rescued ambled up behind me and pressed its head against my heart, thanking me for saving its life.

One bright spring day, twenty years before I rescued that drowning moose calf, Walter and I watched as a grizzly bear charged a cow moose, driving her away from her defenseless newborn calf. The mother watched helplessly from a distance as the bear mauled her calf to death. In my revulsion and rage at such brutality and ugliness, I raised my rifle to shoot the murderous bear. I wanted to kill it so bad I was almost shaking. But before I could pull the trigger, Walter pushed away the barrel.

"Just because you disagree with the bear's actions, does not mean it was wrong or immoral. He just sees things differently than you."

That day I learned that my worldview and cultural perspective is not the only one, nor is it the right one. It is simply one way of seeing things.

Living Mindfully

Knowing that life is full of suffering, despair, disappointment, heartbreak, pain, loss, and grief, I
once asked His Holiness the Dalai Lama during a
talk he gave at the Church of St. John the Divine in
Manhattan: "What is the meaning of life?" Without
blinking, he replied, "Life is hard. There is much
suffering. But you must try to find your own happiness. But remember that others are looking for
their own happiness as well." Even the founders
of America understood this. That's why they included the phrase "and the pursuit of happiness"
in the Constitution. The secret of life is to find
what makes you happy and to allow others the
freedom to do the same.

Be wary of anyone who tells you they know what's best for you. Equally, be wary of thinking that you know what is best for others. Both are contrary to humility.

The more I learn, the more I realize I don't know anything. One way to increase your happiness in life is to admit that you don't know as much as you think you do. When you think you know everything, it is impossible to learn anything.

"The only wisdom is in knowing that you know nothing."
    —Plato

A wise man once said that there are three major problems with humanity: racism, poverty, and ignorance. Racism can be overcome by love, compassion, and tolerance. Poverty can be overcome by sharing. And ignorance can be overcome by learning.

"Ignorance: the root and stem of every evil."
    —Plato

We are all strangers to our own inner desires and selfishness. If you do not know yourself, how can you know anyone else? If you are false to yourself, how can you be true to others? If you do not love yourself, how can you love others?

When asked about the meaning of life, Albert Einstein replied, "We exist for our fellow man."

Elevating oneself above others (vanity) is the root of separation and alienation.

All of my professional career, I have known egotistical professors who think the world revolves around them. Yet, a couple blocks from campus no one has ever heard of them. Learn to control your ego.

Hippocrates, the father of medicine, gave us the phrase, "You are what you eat." He understood that nutritious food is good medicine. Healthier living begins with healthier eating.

Once again, America is rated the fattest nation in the world. The American Medical Association reported in 2018 that almost half of all American adults are obese and that 86,000,000 Americans are pre-diabetic! That's nearly one-third of the population. Part of our poor health can be blamed on the food industry, which has deceived us through marketing and lobbying for decades, padding its wallet at the expense of our deteriorating health. Take for example portion size. When my family goes out to a restaurant, one meal feeds all three of us, with left-overs for our dog when we get home. This is how it evolved: many years ago, one burger joint sold as a meal a regular, one-eighth pound burger patty with a small pile of French fries and a small soda pop. In order to out-compete with that restaurant, the burger joint down the street offered for the same price a quarter-pound burger with twice the pile of fries and a larger cup of soda. Eventually, in order to compete for your business, restaurants offered half-pound and even one pound double and triple-patty monster burgers with a wheel barrow load of deep-fried, oil-soaked fries and a bath tub-sized soda pop. The server-cashier asked if you wanted your meal "Super-Duper Sized" and we smiled and said sure. (They might as well call it "Stupid Sized.") Some diner chains call their enormous breakfast with two or three of everything the "Home Run Slam" platter, because it's enough food to fill four plates. Later, we complain to our concerned doctors, "But Doc, I only had a normal breakfast and a burger and some fries for lunch." Eat smaller portions. Avoid processed foods. Eat less meat. Eat more green vegetables and fruit. Avoid soda pop altogether. Drink more water. Have compassion for your body.

There's a reason they call it fast-food: It speeds you on your way to poor health.

Use smaller plates and bowls. Trick your mind in how it perceives portion size.

Could it be that obesity and loneliness are related? Could it be that many people try to fill the emptiness they feel inside with food?

A recent global study found that poor dietary habits—
not to be confused with malnutrition—is responsi-
ble for more deaths per year than smoking.

At the grocery store check-out line, I watch in dis-
belief as some people fill carts with cases of soda
pop, hang six-packs over the sides of the cart.
Ever read the label on a soda? Not one thing listed
is food. Just because you can put something in
your mouth and swallow it doesn't mean it is food
for the body.

My wife has taught me to read labels on food packaging. If the ingredients are not recognizable as
food, I don't buy it. She also taught me to avoid
the middle aisles of grocery stores where everything is over-processed to increase shelf-life. If you
don't believe me, look at the sodium (salt) content
in a can of soup, a carton of broth, a package of
Ramen noodles, or a can of Spaghettios Beefaroni,
or Ravioli.

If you were the custodian of a church, synagogue,
temple, or mosque, wouldn't you do a good job
taking care of it? Your body is a temple. Be a better caretaker.

"If we eat with moderation, eating only the food
we need and eating the foods that help our bodies to be strong and healthy, then we are showing
love and respect for our bodies and for the Earth."
　　　—Thich Nhat Hanh

"Nothing survives without food, including love."
　　　—Buddha

I do most of the cooking in my family. I especially
love to make healthy soups. I must have over a
thousand recipes. I listen to music while cutting
vegetables. I drink a little wine and dance. I am
happy. Maybe that's why delicious food is said to
be made with love.

In our hectic lives of running from one thing to
the next, too many people treat getting nourish-
ment the same way as they treat filling their car
with gas. How often do you eat while driving in
your car? Slow down while you eat. Turn off the
television. Sit at a table. Listen to relaxing music.
Set aside your anxious thoughts about work. Eat
slowly and mindfully. Be grateful for your food.
Think about where it came from. Enjoy the taste
and sensation. Let mealtime be a sanctuary.

Every year, Americans pop more than eight billion pick-me-up amphetamine and methamphetamine stimulants like Adderall and Ritalin. American doctors prescribe them like candy to children and adults alike. Big Pharma rakes in billions in profits. One of the most cited reasons people abuse the drugs is that they allow them to "get more work done" (recall Ben Franklin's "Time is money"), whether in school or at work. It's a never-ending treadmill of abuse. If everyone else at school or work uses these stimulants, then people clamor for more to "give them an edge over the competition." It has been variously reported that many students in American universities are on one or more of these drugs. One of the side effects is loss of sleep. Remember when a good diet and eight hours of sleep got us through our day just fine? I'd wager that most of the doctors prescribing these drugs did not take them when they earned their medical degrees at highly competitive universities.

More than 75% percent of all communication is non-verbal. Some say the number is more like 90%. That is to say your actions speak louder than words. If you say you are a good person, whom have you helped today?

The Secret of Success: Falling down and getting up, falling down and getting up again. Every successful person knows this to be true. Thomas Edison had hundreds of failures on his way to perfecting the light bulb.

One principle of Buddhism is that all life is suffering. We all struggle or suffer at some time. Do not wish to avoid strife. We are strengthened from the experience. Ernest Hemingway once said that when we break, the broken place mends stronger than it was before.

"Someone I loved once gave me a box of darkness. It took me years to understand that this, too, was a gift."
        –Mary Oliver

It is impossible to be happy when you are always comparing what you have to what everyone else has. Envy only leads to resentment and dissatisfaction. Do not let envy steal your happiness.

John Lennon of The Beatles once said that when he was a schoolboy the teacher asked everyone in class to write down what they wanted to be in life. While other children wrote things like doctor, veterinarian, astronaut, teacher, fireman, etc. John wrote: "Happy." Dumbfounded, the teacher confronted John, telling him he simply didn't understand the nature of the assignment, to which John replied, "You don't understand the nature of life."

Like you, I am not proud of everything I have said or done in my life. In over half a century, I have amassed a litany of wrongs I have perpetrated against others—some intentionally, some unintentionally. But like me, you can learn from your errors, admit that you were wrong, and try to change who you will be today and tomorrow. It is never too late to be a better person.

Every new day is the best day to wake up and decide you are going to have a great day.

Wealth and power can turn even a saint into a sinner. It can transform the kindest person into the cruelest, the most steadfast into the most capricious, and the most generous into the most selfish.

A mind is like a flower. If it is not open, it cannot blossom. The same can be said of the heart.

Everyone I have ever met believes themselves
to be righteous and good—the "Good Guy." They
profess to be imitators of Jesus, Buddha, Muhammad, or some saint. They justify all their actions
on such belief. And yet the world is full of heart-
lessness, cruelty, corruption, bigotry, bullying, tyr-
anny, and evil. It is the Great Conceit of Humanity.

It has always amazed me how the qualities we say
we most admire are kindness, generosity, selfless-

ness, honesty, patience, and understanding; and
the qualities we most abhor are greed and cov-
etousness, meanness, bullying, egotism and selfishness. And while we may admire the qualities of
the first, we adore—even idolize—the fruits of the
second.

Humanity has an unrelenting capacity to justify
even our worst actions or inactions.

Joy has many enemies. Perhaps the most incipient
is our modern predilection for busyness, for always
going a hundred miles an hour in a hundred different directions, as if being busy is a virtue. It is
one of our most persisting illusions. Learn to slow
down, enjoy the present moment. Live fully in every minute for it never comes again.

You've heard it said before, but its importance
bears repetition: What a person projects outwardly
can mask who they are on the inside. Beauty can
conceal great ugliness. Conversely, great beauty
can be masked by ugliness on the outside.

Perhaps our greatest fear, the risk of rejection, is
to show others who we really are.

We tell children the legend of George Washington cutting down the cherry tree to illustrate that telling the truth is an important virtue, yet we elect politicians who lie thousands of times a year. When did lying become a virtue? The normalization of lying presents a profound danger to the fabric of society.

A society that cannot abide the truth cannot abide itself.

Steve Jobs, co-founder of Apple, once said, "We're born, we live for a brief instant, and we die. It's been happening for a long time. Technology is not changing it much … if at all."

Despite technological, medical, and pharmaceutical advances, the average life expectancy of Americans has decreased in recent years.

Technology has its place, but not at the expense of living more fully in the brief time you are allotted.

"No one here gets out alive."
    —Jim Morrison

I vividly remember the night I lay in my bed at seven years old looking at stars outside the window with a dawning realization that the span of my life would be nothing more than an eyeblink to the universe. I realized that I had never known and would never know a time when I did not exist—not the far past or the far future. The galaxy would turn with or without me. It terrified me. So young, I already understood that we only have this moment—the closest we ever come to glimpsing eternity.

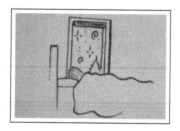

My late friend Carl Sagan, who understood the vastness of the universe more than almost anyone else on Earth, once told me, "Love makes the immensity of the universe bearable."

Some people spend so much of their life focused on their ambitious careers that they forget to live their life and to love the people in their life. I'm reminded of Harry Chapin's 1970s hit song, "The Cat's in the Cradle," in which a busy father never has time for his son, who grows to be just like his father. What behavior are we modeling for our children?

"You don't choose a life; you live one."
    —Emilio Estevez in *The Way*

There's a saying that a single lit candle can light a million candles without diminishing its brilliance. Be a light in an otherwise darkening world. Let the radiance of your love set a million other lives ablaze.

Just as the flame of love can be set ablaze in others, so too can the incinerating inferno of hate. Imagine the sight of an angry mob brandishing guns, pitchforks, and torches. A single torch may have ignited all the others.

Let go of the life you thought you would live so you can start living the life that waits around the corner.

The subatomic particles of the atom, the spinning galaxies, nanoseconds and eons .... The very large and the very small. Without and within is a universe.

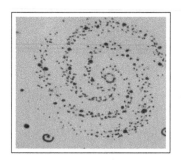

"I contain multitudes." —Walt Whitman

I once drove with a friend across several states. He never stopped talking. I once watched a father smack his child for dropping her ice cream cone. And in a small Midwest town barbershop, I witnessed two White barbers serve only the White customers while ignoring a young, Black college student who came in first. From the first occasion I learned the necessity of silence. From the second, I learned the need for compassion. And from the barbers, I learned tolerance. Life teaches us many lessons.

Be careful what you wall in and what you wall out.

Everything changes. Nothing stays the same. Seas dry up and vanish. Mountains erode. Even the people in our lives change—their coming and going teaches us how to let go. There is nothing to fear from change.

Mark Twain said, "The two most important days in your life are the day you are born and the day you find out why." People always wonder, "What is the meaning of my life?" You were born to give love and to open yourself to receiving love.

Everyone believes they are wonderful, honest, kind, trustworthy, decent, courageous, non-judgmental, selfless, righteous, tolerant, and color blind. If we were all these things why is the world so full of suffering, alienation, and oppression? For most of us, all we see is the mask we wear on the outside. Few of us ever know who we really are on the inside.

Every gardener knows that even seeds dropped unintentionally can take root and grow wherever they fall. What seeds are you unintentionally sowing?

Help Spread the Word

If you loved this book, if it affected you deeply, please help spread the word. Give it to friends and relatives, young and old alike, as a gift. Write a book review for your local newspaper, radio station, or favorite magazine. Post a review on amazon.com or goodreads.com or elsewhere. Talk about the book on Facebook. Tweet about it. Post a YouTube video. Send an Instagram of the book cover. Ask your local librarian to recommend it. Ask your local bookseller to order it. Discuss it in book clubs or study groups. The success of a book depends on readers like you who recommend it to their friends.

About the
Author & Artist

John Smelcer, PhD is the author of more than fifty books, including his poignant retelling of Jesus's crucifixion, *The Gospel of Simon*. Dr. Smelcer studied literature at Cambridge and Oxford and religions at Harvard. In 2015, Dr. Smelcer "discovered" the worldly possessions of Thomas Merton, one of the most influential religious figures and social justice and peace activists of the Twentieth Century. Dr. Smelcer is the inaugural writer-in-residence at the Charter for Compassion, established by Karen Armstrong (*A History of God*), where he teaches a global online course on Poetry for Inspiration and Well-Being. Learn more at www.johnsmelcer.com

Michael T. Duncan studied music at Truman State University in Kirksville, Missouri. Father, husband, and avid outdoorsman, Michael loves doing spray art, painting, and tattoos. He is working on his first children's picture book.